Easy Affordable Cooking 2021

Get Cooking with Debbie G

Easy Affordable Cooking 2021

Get Cooking with Debbie G

I dedicate my book to my parents Ebbie Gatson and Bulah Steven Gatson (RIP 2015) who were married 61 years and always taught me to put God first while be self sufficient. I grew up with 16 Aunts, 5 uncles and 101 1st cousin's , and my mom Bulah was an excellent cook. To my daughter Erin who I drove crazy cooking, who is always supportive, loving, and my best critic!! It takes a village and here are my 1st cousins: Hattie Lewis Booker and Claudia Denise Gatson who from day one were liking and sharing my videos and pictures with our relatives and friends, Robert Samuel from New York, Jason Pryor from Beaumont Texas, Pastor Cemie Clayton from Flagstaff Arizona, Marshall Steven from Rayne Louisiana and cousin Kelly Lewis from Houston Texas who have always supported Get Cooking with Debbie G. To my besties Kathy Temple Bledsaw & MMRH who motivated me to start my cooking channel in March 2021. Watching my Mom and Aunties from Louisiana, and my play mom Rose Johnson was a driving force to me cooking since the 6th grade. I took Home Economics in High School and my HECE teacher and mentor Mrs. Davis was an awesome motivator guiding me to NTSU, now the University of North Texas,. My love of cooking had me selling dinners on Sundays working my way through college obtaining my first degree, BS in Home Economics. Working in Corporate Anerica with SWBYPS & AT&T Management 27 years while obtaining my MS, MBA, and Doctoral studies, never stopped me from cooking for my family, friends, AKA Sorors, and my teams. I have been cooking long before COVID and my recipes are inexpensive, timely, and cost effective. All the recipes in my cookbook were prepared by me along with actual pictures of the cooking posting on Instagram. Over 97% of my recipes have videos. Enjoy Get Cooking with Debbie G, Facebook videos, and Instagram pictures!! Follow, Like, Share fb.me/debbiesquickfoods/d

Contributors

Get Cooking by Debbie G
Get Cooking with Debbie G
Get Cooking with Debbie Gatson

Table of Contents

Recipe Symbol Key

Favorite ★
Time Saver 🕒

Appetizers & Beverages

SPICE GUIDE

Keep spices in tightly covered containers, in a cool dry place. After about a year, spices tend to lose flavor so more may be needed for seasonings. Overheating can cause spices to turn bitter. During lengthy cooking, add spices during the last half hour of cooking time. Usually 1 teaspoon of dried herb equals 1 tablespoon of fresh.

ALLSPICE:	*A blend of cinnamon, cloves and nutmeg.* Meat dishes, egg dishes, fish, gravies, pickles, relishes, tomato sauce, fruit preserves.
BASIL:	*Pungent, sweet aroma.* Broiled and roasted meats and poultry, fish, egg dishes, soups, vegetables, tomato dishes, pasta, dressings, sauces.
BAY LEAF:	*Strong flavor.* Stews, soups, vegetables, pickles, gravies, sauces, marinades.
CAYENNE:	*Red pepper, very hot.* Meats, seafoods, egg and cheese dishes, soups, sauces, dips, spreads, French dressing.
CHILI POWDER:	*Hot, peppery blend of herbs and spices.* Spanish or Mexican dishes, bean and rice dishes, barbeque and cocktail sauces, spreads, dressings, dips, egg dishes, vegetables.
CINNAMON:	*Sweet, spicy aroma.* Breads, cookies, cakes, desserts, pastries, beverages, sauces, vegetables.
CLOVES:	*Strong, spicy-sweet aroma.* Pork and lamb dishes, barbeque sauce, pickles, relishes, fruits, breads, cakes, cookies, desserts.
CUMIN:	*Strong, slightly bitter, lemon flavor.* Spanish, Mexican and Eastern dishes, stews, pickles, tomato dishes.
CURRY:	*A blend of many spices; warm and sharp to hot and spicy.* Meat, seafood, egg and cheese dishes, soups, sauces, seafood, salads, dips.
DILL SEED:	*Mild, slight caraway-like flavor.* Meats, poultry, fish, seafood, stews, soups, salads, sauces, dressings, dips, pickles, breads, egg dishes.
GINGER:	*Pleasant odor, pungent taste.* Oriental dishes, meats, vegetables, fruits, salad dressings, pickles, jams, marinades, breads, desserts.
MARJORAM:	*Spicy, sweet aroma.* Roasted meats and poultry, fish and seafood, egg dishes, stews and casseroles, soups, vegetables, salads, gravies.
MUSTARD:	*Pungent taste.* Pickles, relishes, salad dressings, sauces, dips, egg dishes, marinades, pork and ham, corned beef.
NUTMEG:	*Warm, sweet, spicy flavor.* Vegetables, egg dishes, beverages, breads, cookies, cakes, desserts, sauces.
OREGANO:	*Strong and aromatic.* Italian dishes, pizza and pasta, broiled and roasted meats, fish and seafood, stews and casseroles, egg dishes, tomato sauces, soups, vegetables, salads, salad dressings.
PAPRIKA:	*Varies from mild, slightly sweet to hot; adds color to many dishes.* Meats, poultry, salad dressings, dips, vegetables, soups and salads.
PARSLEY:	*Mild flavor.* Brings out the flavor of most non-sweet foods.
ROSEMARY:	*Sweet, spicy, pine-like fragrance.* Roasted meat and poultry, fish, stews, casseroles, stuffings, salads, breads, egg dishes.
SAGE:	*Strong, slightly bitter.* Roasted meats and poultry, fish, stuffings, vegetables, cheese dishes, salads, gravies, sauces.

Peach Pecan Waffles

Get Cooking with Debbie G

2 cups flour
1 3/4 cup half& half
2 eggs
1/3 cup oil
1/2 cups pecans
1/2 cup peach preserves
2 strips bacon

Mix ingredients and pour half cup at a time into waffle iron. Crumble bacon as desired. 45 min Video on fb 4/7/21 Get Cooking with Debbie G.

Walmart Chicken Salad

Get cooking with Debbie G

2 cans Great value chicken breast 2/$3.98
1 Apple cored and diced
1 cup dried cranberries
1/2 cup chopped walnuts
1 16 ounce vanilla yogurt
1/3-1/2 cup Hellman's Mayo

Optional green onions

Mix all wet ingredients. Then mix in walnuts and cranberries adding in diced chicken. Season with salt and pepper to taste. Garnish with green onions and cranberries. Serve on bed of lettuce or crackers. My gf Kathy eats hers on half an avocado. Enjoy fb video 9/28/21 Get Cooking with Debbie G

Cajun Waffles

Get Cooking with Debbie G

1/4 cup butter
1/4 cup sausage
1/4 cup crap meat
1/3 cup whole kernel corn
1/2 cup Shrimp
1/4 bag (powder) onion mushroom soup mix added to 1/2 cup water
1 tsp oyster flavor sauce
I tsp honey
Store bought or 4 homemade waffles

Sauté butter sausage and corn. After 5 min add shrimp then after 4 min add onion mushroom soup and oyster sauce then add 1 tsp honey. When complete spoon mixture on hot waffles and serve warm. Garnish with sliced tomatoes and sliced apples Video on fb 4/28/21. Get Cooking with Debbie G

Quick Protein Breakfast Fried Rice

Get Cooking with Debbie G

1 cup brown rice
2 stems Bokchoy
1/4 yellow onion chopped
1 cup diced sweet potato
1/2 cup mushrooms
1 tsp fresh minced garlic
1 tsp sesame oil
2 tsp oyster sauce
2 TB Low sodium soy sauce
5-6 clean raw deveined shrimp
1 egg

Mix your seasoning and cook veggies mushrooms and diced sweet potatoes in olive oil. When soft add in sesame oil, oyster sauce, soy sauce, and shrimp, cook 5 min. Plate all, then fry or scramble egg and place on top. Enjoy video fb 9/27/21 Get Cooking with Debbie G

Blackened Turkey Mango Habanero Burger

Get Cooking with Debbie G

2 pounds of Turkey
1/2 cup mango habanero salsa
1/4 cup dried cranberries
1-2 TB garlic powder
1-2 TB Goya Adobe All Purpose Seasoning
1-2 TB Hellmans Creamy Chili Honey Sauce
1/2 TB flour

1/2 cabbage
1/4 onion
1/2 Tb Oil

Combine all the ingredients in first half of ingredients listed above. Form patties and pan fry with 1-2 TB of olive oil. Cook 3/4 minutes each side on Med heat, place on paper towels. Make cabbage slaw with bottom half of ingredients listed above. Cook with minimal olive oil and pan fry until soft, season to your taste.

35 Min Wings (28.5k views) 🕒

Get Cooking with Debbie G

10-12 Wings
1/2 cup olive oil
1/4 cup paprika
1/2 cup cajun seasoning
1/4 cup onion powder
1/4 cup garlic powder
2 large potatoes
1 sm bag carrots
1 yellow onion

Dice your onion and Coat your Pyrex dish with 1/2 olive oil and the onions. Wash your wings and season with paprika, Cajun seasoning, onion, and garlic powders. Cut your potatoes in chunks. I wash my potatoes leaving skin on. Place potatoes in between the seasoned chicken and also place carrots around chicken. Sprinkle onion and garlic powders and place in oven at 460 degrees for 35 minutes. Enjoy video 3/16 fb Get Cooking with Debbie G with over 28.5 k (thousand) views

My Very Easy 35 min Wings

23.9K Views

Fried Chicken Tenders & Fried Corn 1.9k views 🕒

Get Cooking with Debbie G

3 chicken breast
1 bottle hot sauce
1 jar grey poupon mustard
4 cups flour
1 gallon plastic bag
4 corn on the cob
1 egg
1 cup milk
2 Tb garlic salt
1 Tb pepper

Cut Breast into tender size strips and soak 2-3 hours in the mustard and hot sauce. Add 4 cups flour to plastic bag and Drop strips in flour. Shake bag. Drop the strips in hot grease and cook 4 min each side until golden brown. Place on paper towels, Beat egg in milk and put corn on cop in mixture. Add the seasoning into the flour bag and add corn. Shake bag and put in mixture again and place in flour. Fry the cobs 3-4 min each side until golden brown. Also place on paper towels to absorb access grease. Video 5/6/21 on fb with 1.1K views Get Cooking with Debbie G

Number of Servings: 4

Prep Time: 2-3 hours soaking tenders

Homemade Pizza/Pasta Primevera, 12K views ◷

Get Cooking with Debbie G

1 ultra thin pizza crust
1 cup pizza or spaghetti sauce
2 cups mozzarella cheese (or your favorite cheese)
1 pkg pepperoni
1/4 cup purple onions
1/2 cup red yellow and green bell peppers cut in strips
(you can use mushroom or anchovies)

Pasta
1 pkg wheat pasta
1 can lemon sparkling water
your fav veggies, broccoli, 3 cut up bell peppers(all colors), mushrooms, tomatoes and purple onions and shredded carrots

Take your pizza crust and coat with sauce, then add layer of cheese, then layer your veggies and pepperoni, then another layer of cheese. Place in oven set timer 10 min at 425 degrees. Heat iron skillet with 2-3 TB grapeseed oil on medium, add your veggies to saute, as they cook down about 5 min add 1/2 can lemon sparkling water vs broth for less calories or add broth. After they cook down add your tomatoes and shredded carrots. so you still have a little crunch. Its complete, you can even add shrimp or chicken to your pasta. In ten minutes your pizza timer goes off so take pizza out of the oven. Your pizza and pasta are ready, Enjoy!!Video 4/14/21 has 0ver 12k(thousand)views on facebook. Get Cooking with Debbie G

Number of Servings: 3-4

Prep Time: 15 minutes

DEBBIE'S DELICIOUS DIS

Bread and Muffins

MICROWAVE COOKING HINTS

To speed cooking and promote even heating, use the following techniques:

- Stir food during cooking to bring the heated outside parts to the center.
- Turn food over when microwaving small items like hamburgers or chops, or when defrosting.
- Rearrange foods or individual items during cooking to promote even heating.
- Allow standing time to complete the cooking of roasts and baked products.
- Cover foods to hold in moisture and speed cooking.
- Arrange foods in a ring or circular shape to allow maximum exposure to microwave energy. Place tender or thin parts in the center and thicker pieces toward the outside.
- Rotate or move food a quarter or half turn during cooking to allow foods which cook quickly to cook evenly.
- Select foods or pieces of the same size and shape because small items cook faster than large ones.
- Food at refrigerator temperature takes longer to cook than food at room temperature.
- Dense foods take more time to heat than light or porous foods.

Banana Nut Bread ★

Get Cooking with Debbie G

Banana bread Mix (purchased Walmart by butter)
3 ripe bananas
1/3 cup water
1 egg

Optional
1 cup walnuts
1/2 cup brown sugar

Lightly spray Bakers Joy in your pan. Mix all ingredients and pour in pan. Cook at 350 fir 45-50 minutes, checking progress every 20 minutes.
Very easy. No video needed. Fb 10/06/21 Get Cooking with Debbie G

Crawfish Stuffed Pistoles 800 views

Get Cooking with Debbie G

I bag Brown & Serve Rolls
1 bag Precooked Crawfish
1 cup celery & diced onions
2 TB Olive Oil
1/2 cup diced tomatoes
1/2 Tsp oyster flavored sauce
2 TB Brown sugar
1 cup heavy whipping cream

Preheat oven 400
Sauté veggies in olive oil. Add tomatoes & tomato paste and brown sugar. Add 1/2 to 1 cup heavy whipping creme. Simmer till thicken. Cut holes out of rolls then put in stuffing. Place stuffed rolls into greased Pyrex dish. Place remaining stuffing over rolls snd Bake 8-10 min. Watch closely for rolls to brown. Enjoy video 3/25/21 on fb Get Cooking with Debbie G.

Debbie's
DINER

Soups, Stews, Salads and Sauces

CONVERSION OF PAN AND UTENSIL SIZES

UTENSIL	*Measure (Volume)*	*Measure (cm)*	*Measure (inches)*
Baking or cake pan	2 L	20 cm square	8-inch square
	2.5 L	23 cm square	9-inch square
	3 L	30x20x5	12x8x2
	3.5 L	33x21x5	13x9x2
Cookie sheet		40x30	16x12
Jelly roll pan	2 L	40x25x2	15x10x3/4
Loaf pan	1.9 L	23x13x7	9-1/4x5-1/4x2-3/4
Round layer cake pan	1.2 L	20x4	8x1-1/2
			9x1-1/2
Pie pan	750 mL	20x3	8x1-1/4
	1 L	23x3	9x1-1/4
Tube pan	2 L	20x7	8x3
	3 L	23x10	9x4
Springform pan	2.5 L	23x6	9x3
	3 L	25x8	10x4
Baking dish	1 L		1 qt.
	1.5 L		1-1/2 qt.
	2 L		2 qt.
	2.5 L		2-1/2 qt.
	3 L		3 qt.
	4 L		4 qt.
Custard cup	200 mL		6 fl. oz.
Muffin pans	40 mL	4x2.5	1.5x1
	75 mL	5x3.5	2x1-1/4
	100 mL	7.5x3.5	3x1-1/2
Mixing bowls	1 L		1 qt.
	2 L		2 qt.
	3 L		3 qt.

Three Bean Chili Soup

Get Cooking with Debbie Gatson

2 lbs ground Turkey
1 pkg McCormick Hot Chili Seasoning Mix
1TB Basil
1 Box Beef Broth
3 cans of your fav beans (black,red,pinto)
1 can whole kernel Corn
1 can Rotel tomatoes or 1 can Hot Salsa

Pan fry/sauté ground Turkey until cooked. Drain excess oil. Add all ingredients together in large pot, and cook 15-25 min. Enjoy!!

Fresh Fruit Salad

Get Cooking with Debbie G

Fresh fruit
1 container blueberries
1 container strawberries
1 small pineapple cut in chunks
4-5 kiwi peeled and cut in pieces
1/2 cup honey
2TB lime juice

Cut fruit if needed and mix all fruit together
Mix 1/2 cup honey with 2TB lime juice and drizzle over fruit and chill for 30 min to one hour allowing honey to saturate. Enjoy fb 6/13/21 Get Cooking with Debbie G

Homemade Spaghetti Sauce from Scratch

Get Cooking with Debbie G

1-2 lbs ground meat
1 large red onion
1 small celery
1 can Campbell's tomatoes soup
1 can Rotel
1/3 cup garlic powder
1 cup tomato sauce
2 TB ea Oregano & Italian seasoning
1/3 cup brown sugar
1 pkg pasta

Prepare pasta and set to the side. Brown your ground meat with diced red onions and diced celery. Drain excess oil and place back in skillet.In quart pot mix soup, Rotel. garlic powder, tomato sauce, oregano, Italian seasoning, and brown sugar. Cook on med-high for ten minutes. Be careful it splatters. Add your meat cook addtl 20 min. Sauce is ready to pour over pasta. Enjoy video 9/10/21 fb Get Cooking with Debbie G

Three Bean Chili Soup & Fruit Salad

Get Cooking with Debbie G

2 pounds ground Turkey
1 pkg McCormick Hot Chlil Seasoning mix
1 TB Basil
1 box beef broth
3 cans of your fav beans (black,red,pinto)
1 can whole kernel corn
1 can Rotel
1/2 water melon
1 can sliced peaches in syrup
1 can pineapple
2 cups grapes(halfed)
2 small apples

Pan fry turkey in pan with 1 pkg McCormick seasoning, and basil. Discard grease, set aside. In large pot mix broth entire contents of all cans beans, corn and Rotel. Add cooked turkey to the pot. For salad mix all fruit together. If using fresh fruit sprinkle lemon juice to prevent browning. Enjoy video 5/27/21 fb Get Cooking with Debbie G

Main Courses: Beef, Pork and Lamb

EQUIVALENTS AND SUBSTITUTIONS

1 pound shelled walnuts	=	3 cups chopped walnuts
1 pound raisins	=	2-3/4 cups seedless raisins
1 pound dates	=	2-1/2 cups pitted dates
1 tablespoon cornstarch	=	2 tablespoons flour or 4 teaspoons tapioca
1 medium clove of garlic	=	1/8 tsp. garlic powder
1 cup honey	=	1 cup molasses or corn syrup
1 cup ketchup	=	1 cup tomato sauce plus 1/2 cup sugar plus 2 table-spoons vinegar
1 teaspoon dry mustard	=	1 tablespoon prepared mustard
1 small onion	=	1 tablespoon dried onion
1 cup tomato juice	=	1/2 cup tomato sauce plus 1/2 cup water
1 cup self-rising flour	=	1 cup flour plus 1-1/2 tablespoons baking powder plus 1/2 teaspoon salt
1 egg	=	1 teaspoon cornstarch
1 cup liquid honey	=	1-1/4 cups sugar plus 1/4 cup liquid
1 cup corn syrup	=	1 cup sugar plus 1/4 cup liquid
1 cup buttermilk	=	1 cup plain yogurt
1 cup sour cream	=	1 cup plain yogurt
1 cup tomato juice	=	1/2 cup tomato paste plus 1/2 cup water

Memorial Day BBQ

Get Cooking with Debbie G

Small package of pork chops
Small package of ribs
Two links of sausage

Season Meat with Badia and a little red pepper and place on girl. When almost complete pour on Sweet Baby Rays and smoke another 10 minutes
Enjoy fb 6/2/21 Get Cooking with Debbie G

Memorial Day BBQ

Rump Blade Roast

Get Cooking with Debbie G

1 Rump Blade Roast
Badia Seasoning
Garlic powder
1/4 Hoison ssuce
3 bell peppers, red, yellow and green
1 small bag of red potatoes

Clean your roast and season it with Badia and garlic powder. Use 1/4 Hoison sauce coating top of roast. Lay bell peppers and potatoes around the roast. Put no water or broth, makes its own juice. Cover with foil and cook 360 for 1 hour and 15 minutes. Enjoy video 8/7/21 on fb Get Cooking with Debbie G

Grillmates Pork Ribeyes & Caramelized Carrot Matchsticks

Get Cooking with Debbie G

1 Pkg Pork Ribeyes
1 Pkg Carrot matchsticks
1 jar Grillmates (choose ur fav flavor)
2 Tb Olive oil
1/4 tsp butter
1 TB Badia seasoning
2 tsp cinnamon sugar

Put Tb olive oil in iron skillet. Clean pork ribeyes and season with Grillmates seasoning. Pan fry for ten minutes until ea side is brown. In a smaller skillet add 1/4 tsp butter and 2 cups of matchsticks and cook on medium fir 20 min. Add 1 tsp Badia and 2 tsp cinnamon sugar while cooking an addtl 5 min. Serve all warm. Enjoy video 9/7/21 fb Get Cooking with Debbie G

Beef & Broccoli Stir Fry

Get Cooking with Debbie G

One flank steak (marinated 1 hr in teriyaki)
1/4 cup sesame oil
1 small bag broccoli
1 cup mushrooms
I cup onions
1/4 cup Hoison
1/4 cup oyster sauce

Cut marinated steak into strips (smaller the better)
Pan fry Med in 1/4 sesame oil and 1/4 olive oil. when browned about 5-7 minutes, add mushrooms and onions. When veggies are brown add 1/4 cup Hoison and 1/4 cup oyster sauce. When liquids start a rapid boil cut fire lower and add broccoli cook for another 5 min and let sit 5 min before serving. Enjoy video 5/3/21 on fb with over 600 views. Get Cooking with Debbie G

Fried Ribs

Get Cooking with Debbie G

1 package Ribs
1 cup of Kikkoman
1 cup white cooking wine
Badia seasoning
Cayenne pepper
1 pkg pancake waffle mix
1 gallon plastic bag(freezer or regular)
BBQ Sauce
Salsa

Marinade ribs in 1 cup each of Kikkoman and white cooking wine. Take ribs out of marinade and season with Badia and cayenne pepper. Cut up ribs then shake in bag of mixed pancake/waffle mix and fry them like chicken. Turn while browning to make sure all sides cook about 7/10 min. Then let them sit 4 minutes.Eat with bbq sauce or salsa. Ribs video 5/04/21 on fb
Get Cooking with Debbie G

BBQ Steak Baked Potato

Get Cooking with Debbie G

1 small beef flank steak
1 stick butter
2 Large Potatoes
1/2 cup sour cream
2 tsp chives
1 cup heavy creme
2 Tb Mayo
1 tsp parsley
1/2 tsp Rosemary

Marinate and tenderize your flank steak for 30 min to a hour. I used terrayaki marinade and 1 TB Worcestershire sauce. Cut meat in strips. Cook potatoes in microwave 12-15 min then scoop out the potato into a bowl keeping potato shells in tact. Mix the remaining ingredients with the potatoes and place back into shells. There will be more left after filling the two so you can make an extra bowl for later. Then top potatoes with your meat and Sweet Baby Rays BBQ sauce. Video on fb 3/31/21 with over 770 views. Get Cooking with Debbie G

Main Courses: Seafood, Poultry, Pasta and Casseroles

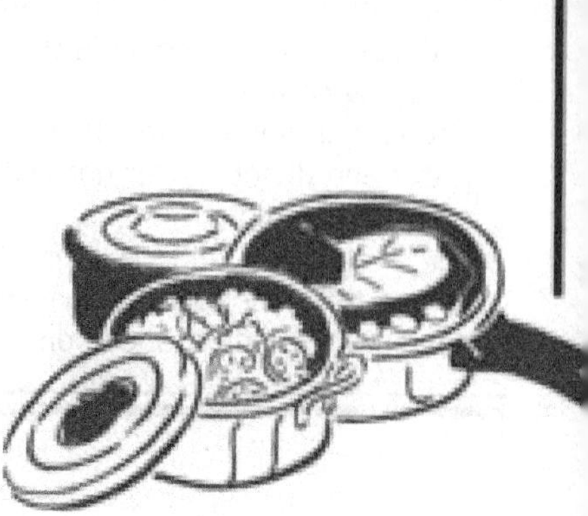

OVEN TEMPERATURE CHART

MISCELLANEOUS	Temp.	Minutes
Custard Cup	300F	20-30
Custard Casserole	300F	45-60
Soufflé	325F	50-60
Timbales	300F	35-45
Rice Pudding	325F	50-60

TABLE FOR DRIED FRUITS

FRUIT	Amount of Sugar or Honey	Cooking Time
Apricots	1/4 c. for each c. fruit	40 min.
Figs	1 tbsp. for each c. fruit	30 min.
Peaches	1/4 c. for each c. fruit	45 min.
Prunes	2 tbsp. for each c. fruit	45 min.

RULES FOR WHIPPING CREAM

- Chill the cream, bowl and beaters in a refrigerator for at least 2 hours. Beat until it is fairly stiff.
- If cream is beaten until it is warmer than 45 degrees, it will turn to butter.
- Should cream start to turn buttery, whip in 2 or 3 more tbsp. of cold milk.
- If you wish the cream to keep stiff for a day or two, add one teaspoon gelatin soaked in one tablespoon cold water. Dissolve the gelatin over hot water; allow to cool to the consistency of egg white before adding to the cream and whipping.
- Use medium speed when whipping cream with an electric beater.
- Cream, when whipped, almost doubles in bulk.

SUBSTITUTES FOR WHIPPING CREAM

1. Use light cream or cereal cream after allowing it to stand undisturbed for 48 hours in the refrigerator. Whip as you would whipping cream.
2. Prepare cream as given above. Soak 1 tsp. gelatin in 2 tbsp. cold water and dissolve over hot water. Allow to cool; then add to the cream and whip.
3. Use evaporated milk. Milk prepared with gelatin holds up better and longer, but may be more convenient to chill it on occasion. Chill 12 hours. Use medium speed on the electric beater when whipping.

Beer Battered Fish/Onion Rings

Get Cooking with Debbie Gatson

Jerk Drums with Jerk Potatoes

Get Cooking with Debbie G

Jerk Drums with Jerk Potatoes

I made my own Jerk seasoning from scratch using 1Tb ea of Onion Powder Garlic Powder dried Parsley & Brown Sugar, 2Tsp each of Cayenne Pepper Smoked Paprika & Seasoning salt, 1 tsp ea. of black pepper Thyme & Allspice with 1/2 tsp ea. of Red pepper flakes Cinnamon Nutmeg & Cumin. Mix your ingredients. Wash your drums and make slits in meat so seasoning sets in and coat both sides. Let them sit 20 min while you Quarter your Russet potatoes also coating them olive oil with Jerk seasoning. Place potatoes in iron skillet middle of oven on high 20 min then place your drums with potatoes for another 20 min on high. Take skillet out if oven add 1 cut water with 1/2 cup Worcester sauce with 1-2 Tb butter and sautéed on medium another 30 min. If your meat is thick you might need another 10 min. Enjoy and watch video on Fb Get Cooking with Debbie G.Happy Saturday

Louisiana BBQ Shrimp

Get Cooking with Debbie G

Number of Servings: 2-3

Prep Time: 30 minutes

Shrimp Veggie Stir Fry

Get Cooking with Debbie G

I pkg of Veggies (broccoli,carrots,cauliflower)
1/2 stick butter
2 TB Olive Oil
1/2 cup Hoisin sauce
1 bag medium shelled deveined raw shrimp

Wok stir fry your veggies in the butter and olive oil. Cook for ten minutes then add Hoison sauce then add shrimp and cook 5 more minutes. Enjoy video on fb 6/06/21 Get Cooking with Debbie G

Cajun Shrimp & Grits

Get Cooking with Debbie G

1 pkg Pioneer Cajun Shrimp mix/seasoning
1 bag large raw shrimp
1 cup green peppers
1 cup red onions
1 cup chopped celery
1 stick of butter
1 can Rotel tomatoes
1 box variety grits

Prepare your favorite grits per instructions.
In a saucepan, melt your stick of butter add green peppers and red onions, sauté on low. Then add pioneer seasoning pkg and Rotel. Let simmer then add shrimp and cook 4-5 min only. Place your Cajun Shrimp over your cheddar grits. Video on fb 8/26/21 Get Cooking with Debbie G.

Kickin Chicken Finger Lickin Wings

Get Cooking with Debbie G

1 pkg of 10-12 wings
1 bottle Soy sauce
1 bottle of Kickin Chicken Finger Lick seasoning
1 stick butter
1/4 cup Hoison sauce
1/4 cup soy sauce
1 indoor grill
1 Medium bag veggies

Clean wings and soak in soy sauce for 30 minutes
Remove wings and season with kickin chicken seasoning and place on grill turning occasionally 39-45 min. Take off grill and plate. While wings are grilling put veggies in microwave dish with one stick butter and sauces. Microwave 15 min. Enjoy
Video fb 7/13/21 Get Cooking with Debbie G

Coconut Battered Shrimp & Red Tatoes

Get Cooking with Debbie G

I sm bag shredded coconut
I sm bag red potatoes
I pig Louisiana Seasoned Beer Battered Mix
Coconut Oil for frying
Badia seasoning
Black pepper seasoning
Sm seltzer water or can of beer

Clean shrimp and mix in Louisiana batter mix (follow directions using seltzer water or beer)add in 1/2 cup shredded coconut. Drop shrimp in hot coconut oil and Fry for 4-5 minutes. Set to the side. Cut your red potatoes in sections, season with Badia and black pepper and fry them in oil. Remove from grease and sprinkle cheese over potatoes. Enjoy video 9/11/21 on fb Get Cooking with Debbie G

Blackened Shrimp Tostado

Get Cooking with Debbie G

Pkg of Crispy Tostados
1 bag of shrimp
Emerils blackened seasoning
1 sm can of black beans
1 container Habanero Mango Salsa
1/2 red onion
Jalapeños
I am can whole kernel corn
1/2 cup Rotel tomatoes
1/2 res bell pepper
Optional chili honey sauce

Pan fry your raw shrimp in Emeril seasoning for 2/3 min on each side. Place on tostada. Chop all bell pepper and layer all the ingredients, whatever your preference on top. Drizzle with salsa and chili honey sauce. Video 9/13 on Facebook. Get Cooking with Debbie G

Delectable Seafood Dirty Rice 3.6k views

Get Cooking with Debbie G

1/2 bag Crawfish (precooked)
1/2 bag crabmeat (real or imitation)
1 bag large or extra large shrimp
1 cup celery
1 cup onions
1 cup bell peppers
1 stick butter
1 can french onion soup
1/2 cup hoison sauce
1/3 cup soy sauce
2 bags success brown rice

Sauté veggies in butter, when soft add in crawfish & crabmeat sauté 5 min. Add French onion and Hoison sauce. Simmer 5 minutes then add shrimp and soy sauce. Cook 5 min then add rice to your preference. Video fb 3/24/21 with 3.6 k (thousand) views. Get Cooking with Debbie G

All Encompassed Fried Rice 3.1K Views

Get Cooking with Debbie G

Video viewed 3.1 k (thousand) views on fb

1 stick of butter
Several corn cobs boiled and seasoned
1 bag shrimp
1-2 cups of onions, bell peppers & green onions
1 rope Cajun sausage
2 chicken breast marinated in 1/2 cup kikoman soy and 1/2 cup hot sauce and cut in small pieces
1/2 cup oyster flavored sauce
1 small pot of cooked rice

Melt butter in wok and sautée your veggies and put chicken in after 15 min then add in sausage. Add in the seasoned corn on cob cut in pieces. Add 1/2 cup oyster sauce.simmer another 5 min then add shrimp once pink then add rice two - three cups. Let it simmer 5 minutes & serve. Enjoy fb 4/19 with 3.1K (thousand) views Get Cooking with Debbie G

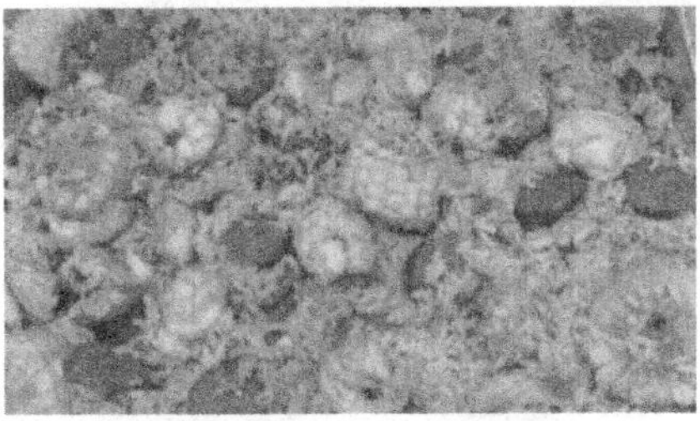

Chicken Fettuccini Alfredo 1.7k views

Get Cooking with Debbie G

I pkg cooked pasta vermicelli
1/4 cup butter
1 1/2 cup heavy Creme
1 1/2 cups fresh Parmesan shredded cheese
1/4 cup fresh diced garlic
1/4 cup chopped green onions
1/4 cup parsley chopped
1/2 tsp Italian seasoning
2 chicken breast

Season your breast with Badia and Roast/broil chicken Breast on medium rack in oven for 20 min. Cook your pasta and place in dish. In sauce pan melt butter, add garlic and green onion on low/ medium then add heavy creme and parsley. Slowly fold in cheese on low fire and after mixture thickens then add sliced breast and pour over pasta. Enjoy fb video 4/8/21 with 1.7 k (thousand) views Get Cooking with Debbie G

Catfish Jambalaya on Rice

Get Cooking with Debbie G

1 pkg Pioneer Jambalaya mix
1 cup water
1 can Rotel
1 cup bell peppers
1/2 cup celery
Badia seasoning
Garlic seasoning
1-2TB flour

Coat wok with olive oil. Sauté bell peppers and celery until softened. Clean catfish and season with Badia and garlic powders place in wok and panfry about 3 min on each side. Then mix pioneer with water and pour over fish along with Rotel and place on med flame for another 5-7 min. If not thick enough you can add TB Flour to water and add to mixture. Cook your rice. Place catfish jambalaya over rice and enjoy. Video 8/26/21 on fb Get Cooking with Debbie G

Iron Skillet Bacon Wrapped Thighs

Get Cooking with Debbie G

Package of Chicken Thighs
1/4 cup Badia Seasoning
Package of Apply Bacon
1 small yellow onion
2 TB garlic powder
I small package of mushrooms
1/4 cup olive
1 pkg of rice or noodles

Warm your iron skillet with 1/4 cup olive oil. Wash your thighs and season with garlic powder. Place the diced yellow onion in skillet. Wrap the thighs with apple bacon and place in skillet.Let them cook 15 min Add mushrooms and cook another 20 minutes until done. If you would like gravy take thighs out and add 1/2 cup of broth and it will make a small gravy. Cook your rice or noodles and top with thighs. Enjoy video on fb 6/07/21 Get Cooking with Debbie G

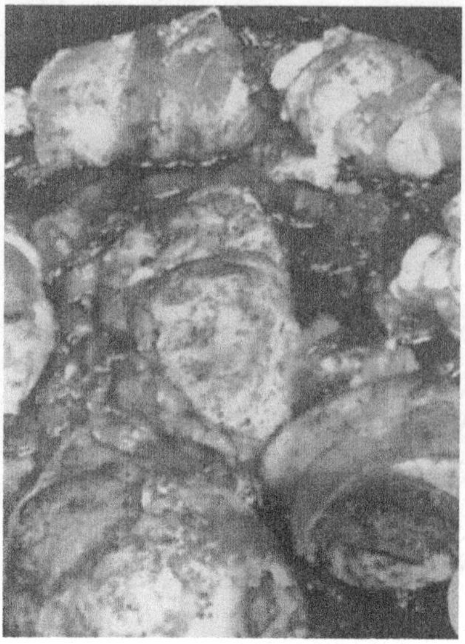

Pineapple Chicken w/Broccoli& Brown Rice

Get Cooking with Debbie G

2 Smoked Chicken Breast
1 can Pineapple chucks with juice
1 TB Flour
1 TB Oil
1 TB Kitchen Bouquet
1 TB Honey
1 sm bag Bricocoli florets
1 cup ea green onions & celery

You can season breast and broil in oven with liquid smoke. Cut up your smoked breast, that's half the flavor.Put 1 TB Oil in wok, add in green onions, celery and broccoli and cook 5 minutes. Mix the 1 Tb flour with kitchen bouquet and add to mixture along with the can of pineapple chucks. Once mixed it will thicken and form a brown roux/gravy. Last add in the chicken breast. You can eat it by itself or add brown rice. Video on fb 8/25/21 Get Cooking with Debbie G

Breakfast Fried Swai with Coucous & Strawberry Salsa

Get Cooking with Debbie G

1 pkg Twisto Couscous
Swai Fillets
Emerils blackened seasoning
Louisiana Orleans fish fry
1 sm pkg strawberries
1/2 Red onion
1 Tb orange or lemon juice

Place your pkg Twisto Couscous in microwave bowl with 2/3 cup water for 2 minutes and set aside. Rinse your Swai fillets and pat dry leaving a lil moisture. Season fillets with Emerils then coat with Louisiana Fish fry. Pan fry in minimum veg oil for 3-4 minutes each side until crispy. Rinse and cut up your strawberries and dice red onions and add 1TB of orange or lemon juice. Mix together in bowl. Plate all and enjoy a low cal breakfast. Video 9/18 on fb. Get Cooking With Debbie G

Beer Base Baked Chicken

Get Cooking with Debbie G

1 whole chicken
1 large can Corona Msngo Citrus beer
1/2 cup olive oil
1/3 cup Badia seasoning
1/4 cup garlic
Dash of red pepper
1/4 cup oh Grillmates seasoning
1 small onion

Soak chicken in beer for 1-2 hours. Cut whole in center of onion and place at top of metal rack.Take chicken out of beer and rub with olive oil. Then rub all seasonings onto the chicken. Stuff chicken on top of grill onto the onion. If no grill you can place chicken in a smoker, or lay it on foil and stuff onion in the chicken and place uncovered in the center of the Oven. I placed the chicken on metal grill and placed in oven uncovered on Med heat at 375 for one hour. Video is on fb 8/30/21 Get cooking with Debbie G

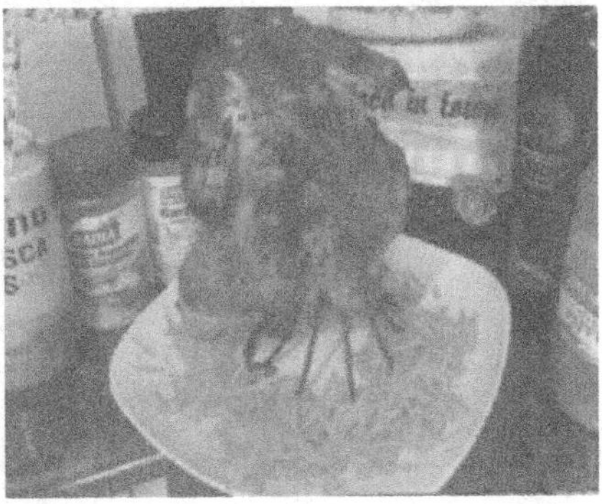

Pecan Crusted Chicken Breast

Get Cooking with Debbie G

2-3 Thick Chicken breast
1 sm pkg pecans
1 cup Dijon mustard
1 cup fresh spinach
Panko crumbs
Sm 6 oz pkg of pecans
3TB Olive oil
2/3 slices provolone cheese

Preheat oven at 435. Put pecans in blender to pulverize, mix with Panko crumbs. Clean your thick breast and slice down center for stuffing. Stuff with spinach and provolone cheese. Cover Breast with Dijon mustard then roll in crumbs. You can secure stuffing with toothpicks. Put olive oil in iron skillet and lightly brown the breast on both sides for 5-7 minutes. Place the entire iron skillet in the oven at 425 for 8-10 minutes. Take out let it sit 5 minutes before cutting. Enjoy video 5/13/21 fb Get Cooking with Debbie G.

Italian Stuffed Sausage Spaghetti

Get Cooking with Debbie G

Pkg of Linguini noodles
1 lb of Italian sausage
Fresh Grated Parmesan cheese
2TB Oregano
1 Jar of Spaghetti Sauce
1 small velveeta cheese

Cook your linguini per instructions. Put to the side.
Mix Parmesan cheese and Oregano into the sausage and firm meatballs by rolling the meat in between your hands. Once ball is formed make a small indenture in the ball and stuff a small piece of velveeta then roll the ball in your hands to enclose the cheese. Fry the meatballs in veg oil on low-Med for 8-10 minutes until cooked. Open your can of sauce and add the balls into the sauce and cook another ten minutes. Pour mixture over your noodles. Top with Parmesan and enjoy. Video 5/28/21 on fb Get Cooking with Debbie G

Bok Choy Shrimp & Noodles

Get Cooking with Debbie G

2 Bok Choy clean and chopped
1 bag x large shrimp
1 medium Ted bell pepper
1/3 cup green onions
2 TB Ginger
1/3 cup oyster sauce
1/3 cup soy sauce
3 TB Butter

Cook noodles or your favorite pasta and set aside.
Soak Bok choy in vinegar & water 15-25 min until clean removing dirt then dry off and chop in pieces.
In saucepan sautee shrimp in butter 3-4 min then remove. Add your green onions, ginger, soy,and oyster sauce then bell peppers adding boy choy last. When it cooks down around 15 min, add your noodles. Add your shrimp last 5 min so not to overcook. Video on fb 4/28/21 Get Cooking with Debbie G

Number of Servings: 4

Prep Time: 45 min

Ranch Wings /Ranch Potatoes

Get Cooking with Debbie G

Pkg if ten wings
I pkg Ranch Seasoning (buy pkg of 4)
3 cups corn starch
I plastic bag for shaking wings & cornstarch
I bottle sweet Babyrays bbq sauce(your flavor)
1 small old if grated cheese (your preference)
1 small bag of red potatoes
1 cup of half & half

Clean your wings and use 1 Pkg of Ranch seasoning to season for every ten wings.Fill your bag with corn starch. Then place a couple wings at a time in your plastic bag filled with corn starch and shake tip coated. Fry wings 5 at a time so they are not crowded and cook till crisp. Cut your red potatoes in half or thirds and season with Ranch seasoning. Put in microwave and cook 10-12 minutes with one cup of half and half or milk. When done melt cheese over potatoes for one minute
Video 5/12/21 on fb Get Cooking with Debbie G

Shrimp & Cheddar Grits 2.2k views

Get Cooking with Debbie G

2 TB Kary Dry Roux
1 cup water
1 bag shrimp
2 pkg Quaker Instant Cheddar Grits
1 cup milk
1 sm container Knorr Chicken Homestyle stock
1 TB Hoison Sauce
1/2 cup diced green onions
2 TB brown sugar
1 TB Thyme
1/2 tsp Badia complete
1/2 stick butter

Saucepan melt butter and sauté green onions. Add 1 cup of water add Kary and add Knorr. Medium heat until it thickens. Add hoison and brown sugar. Then add thyme and Badia. The add shrimp. If sauce is too thin mix 2 TB flour in 1/4 water and add until mixture thickens. Place mixture over your grits and Enjoy. Video on fb Get Cooking with Debbie G on 4/04/21 with 2.2 K (thousand) views

Shrimp Sausage Spaghettini

Get Cooking by Debbie G

1/4 cup oil
1 cup celery
1 cup green onions
1/2 Bag shredded carrots
1/4 cup butter
1 can diced tomatoes
16 oz can tomato paste
1 box whole grain thin spaghetti
1 pkg (3 ropes) Garlic smoked sausage
1 sm bag medium shrimp
1 tsp ea. chives & oregano
1/4 cup honey
1/2 tsp red pepper
1 TB Badia

Sauté veggies 1/4 cup oil medium fire in wok. Add 1/4 cup butter. Add Garlic sausage and cook with veggies. Add 1 can diced tomatoes or Rotel if you want it spicy. Then add can of paste eith 1 csn water. Simmer until it thickens. Then add 1/4 cup honey and 1/2 tsp red pepper. K lol at 5 min add Badia and shrimp. Enjoy video 4/11/21 on fb Get Cooking with Debbie G.

DINER

30 min Jambalaya

Get Cooking with Debbie G

1 rope spicy sausage
1 small Pkg chicken tenders
1 small bag raw shrimp
I stalk green onions
1 small yellow onion
1TB ea Karys Roux, garlic powder,Cajun powder, and d. brown sugar
1 can chicken broth
Cajun powder

Sauté your chopped green onions and yellow onions in your wok with 2 TB olive oil. Then add your chicken tenders(season with cajun powder). Cook about 8-10 min on medium heat turning them every three minutes. Then add your sausage. Cook for another three min. Push meat to one side and add your roux, onion, and garlic powders, then pour in 1 cup of chicken broth. As it thickens stir all together and if you want darker roux you can add another TB of roux, Add in 1 TB of brown sugar and cook another 8-20 min on medium. Enjoy!! Video on Fb Sat 10/2/21.
Get Cooking with Debbie G

Raspberry Walnut Chicken Thighs 1K views

Get Cooking with Debbie G

4 Chicken Thighs
1 cup green onions
1 cub bell peppers
2 TB Olive oil
1/2 cup Worcestershire sauce
1/4 Italian Seasoning
1/4 cup smoked paprika
1 bowl washed fresh spinach
1 small bowl matchstick carrots
1 cup Raspberry Walnut Vinaigrette

If thighs are thick use a knife and cut down center to open then use a metal tenderizer to flatten. You can place a sheet of plastic wrap over meat to prevent blood splatter. Rub smoked paprika, Worcestershire sauce and Italian seasoning on both sides of thighs. Place in iron skillet with minimal olive oil browning all sides 7 minutes. Add more Worcestershire sauce and cook another 5 minutes. Add raspberry vinaigrette then add veggies and cook an addtl 5 min on low heat till veggies are soft and tasty and chicken is done. Video 3/29/21 on fb over 971 views. Get Cooking with Debbie G

Fried Turkey Tacos/Meat Pies 1.3 k views

Get Cooking with Debbie G

I pkg ground Turkey
1 cup celery & 1 cup green onions
1 pls of small flour tortillas
1 pkg pizza or pie crust
1/2 cup Badia
1/2 cup picante sauce
1/2 cup shredded cheese
2TB vegetable
1 egg

Preheat oven 350
Sauté ground Turkey with celery and green onions until cooked. Lay your dough on cutting board or clean counter and use a small bowl to make round impressions or circles. Use your knife to cut out circles making 3-4. Place a line of neat and sauce down center and fold over dough using your fork to secure edges. Beat your egg and brush overdough before placing in oven. Cook10-13 minutes.For fried tacos just place pie shaped dough in hot grease for a couple minutes on each side. When they start floating in grease they are ready. View on fb 3/26/21 with over 1.3k (thousand) views
Get Cooking with Debbie G

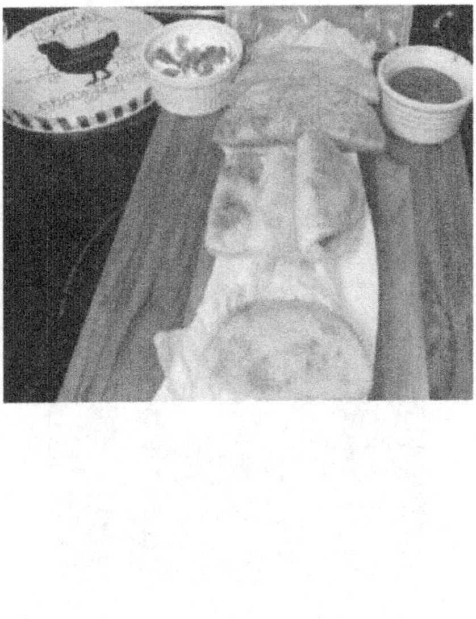

Seafood Quiche Pie

Get Cooking with Debbie G

2 Pie crust
10 raw shrimp
1 can lump crab meat
1 tsp Old Bay seasoning
1/2 tsp ea garlic& onion powders
4 eggs
1/2 cup whipping cream
1/2 cup almond milk
1 cup Pictsweet pepper & onion blend
1 cup fresh mixed cheese

Bake your pie crust 15 min on 350. You can always make one large one using pizza dough on a pizza pan. Put crust aside. Leave oven on. Mix your eggs, milks, and 1/2 cheese and put to the side.Add in raw shrimp and crabmeat. Heat a skillet and sauté your pictsweet. Let it kool and add it to the mixture along with al the seasonings. Then pour half of the mixture into each pie shell. Bake 20 mini, then turn oven down to 295 and bake an additional 20 minutes. Enjoy!! 9/30/21 No video
Get Cooking with Debbie G

Number of Servings: 4

Prep Time: 30 minutes

Chicken Fried Chicken & Corn with Rice 1.9k views

Get Cooking with Debbie G

3-4 Chicken breast
1 stick butter
1 bag of frozen whole kernel corn
1/2 cup green onions
2 TB Badia
2 TB Basil
2 cups flour
1TB baking powder
1 TB corn starch
1 egg

Hot Drizzle glaze- 1/2 cup honey,1 tsp cayenne, 1 tsp parsley

Melt butter and sauté green onions. Add corn cook 15 minutes stirring then add Badia and basil. Add 1/2 cups rice and set aside. Take large breast and with sharp knife cut down center to open to larger breast and tenderize with metal Mallot. Mix flour, baking powder and corn starch in bowl. Beat an egg in separate bowl. Sprinkle Badia or my seasoning (recipe in this book) on the breast and dip in egg mixture then flour and repeat the process. Add 2/4 cup of oil in iron skillet then fry breast browning each side and fry 8-11 minutes on medium heat. Plate all and enjoy video on fb 4/09/21 with 1.9 k (thousand) views Get Cooking with Debbie G

Best food in town
Debbie's
DINER
Best food in town

Mexican Cornbread & Turkey Tacos

Get Cooking with Debbie G

I pkg Jiffy Corn muffins or cornbread from scratch
1 lb Turkey
1 red onions
Badia
1 sm can of corn
Sm cannot Rotel
1 sm cabbage
Sm jar of Salsa
1 sm yellow onion
Jalapeños
Sour cream
Small Flour tortillas

Mix your cornbread. Grease pan for cornbread with non stick spray. Brown your Turkey with red onions and your fav seasoning. I used Badia. Pour 1/2 cornbread batter in pan. Mix and layer over cornbread, 1/3 Turkey (remainder will be used for tacos), 1/3 can of Rotel drained, and 1/3 corn drained. Pour remaining cornbread mixture over the top of the layered ingredients. Place in oven 350 and bake 20-26 minutes until brown. Stick a toothpick down center of cornbread to make sure it is baked. Toothpick should come out dry not milky. Next layer flour tortillas in the taco holder. Add 1.5 TB meat, diced cabbage, salsa, diced onions, and jalapeños. Top with sour cream and enjoy. Mexican cornbread is great with a Salad. Enjoy video 9/12/21 fb Get Cooking with Debbie G

Vegetables and Vegetarian Dishes

SAUCES

WHITE SAUCE	Liquid	Thickening	Fat	Salt
No.1 thin	1 c. milk	1 tbsp. flour	1 tbsp.	1/2 tsp.
No.2 medium	1 c. milk	2 tbsp. flour	1-1/2 tbsp.	1-1/2 tsp.
No.3	1 c. milk	3 tbsp. flour	2 tbsp.	1 tsp.
No.4 thick	1 c. milk	4 tbsp. flour	2-1/2 tbsp.	1 tsp.

Use No.1 sauce for cream soups. Use No.2 sauce for creamed or scalloped dishes or gravy. Use No.3 sauce for soufflés. Use No.4 sauce for croquettes.

VEGETABLE TIMETABLE - MINUTES

VEGETABLE	Boiled	Steamed	Baked
Asparagus Tips	10-15	3-8	
Asparagus, tied in bundles	20-30	6-10	
Artichokes, French	40	45-60	
Bean, Lima	20-40	60	
Bean, String	15-35	60	
Beets, young with skins on	30	60	70-90
Beets, old	60-120	60-120	
Broccoli, florets	5-10	4-5 (al dente)	
Broccoli, stems	20-30	8-10	
Brussels Sprouts	20-30	6-8	
Cabbage, chopped	10-20	5-10	
Cauliflower, stem down	20-30	10-15	
Cauliflower, florets	8-10	5-7	
Carrots, cut across	20-30	40	
Chard	60-90	90	
Celery, 1-1/2 inch pieces	20-30	45	
Corn, green, tender	5-10	15	20
Corn on the cob	8-10	15	
Eggplant, whole	30	40	45
Marrow	15-40		
Onions	25-40	60	60
Parsnips	25-40	60	60-75
Peas, green	5-15	5-15	
Peppers	20-30	30	30
Potatoes, depending on size	20-40	60	45-60
Potatoes, sweet	40	40	45-60
Scalloped potatoes			60-90
Pumpkin, in cubes	30	45	60
Tomatoes, depending on size	5-15	50	15-20
Turnips, depending on size	25-40		

Fast & Easy Sausage Spud

Get Cooking with Debbie G

Large Russet Potato
1/4 stick butter
1/4 diced red onion
1/4 cup Sharp cheddar cheese
Badia

Wash your potato and slice an opening down the center. Microwave your spud (potato) for 8-10 min
Use a small pan and melt your butter adding in red onions and sausage and cook. When potato is done, mash sides to pop open the center. Sprinkle some Badia and add the onion sausage mixture on top. Add shredded cheese on top. Enjoy video 6/10/21 fb Get Cooking with Debbie G

Pan fried Different Cabbage 1.6 k views

Get Cooking with Debbie G

1 small head of cabbage cut in small pieces
1 cup jalapeño sausage
1 cup smoked chicken breast
1 cup diced carrots
2 sticks butter
1 cup bell peppers
1 cup purple onions

Melt butter add bell peppers, purple onions and carrots for ten minutes with sausage. Then add cabbage. Let it cook ten minutes then add cooked smoked chicken breast until cabbage is cooked to your liking. Video received 1.6k (thousand) views. Get Cooking with Debbie G.

Number of Servings: 5

Prep Time: 45 min

Crockpot Red Beans 1.6k views

Get Cooking with Debbie G

Using two medium bags of beans
For each addtl bag add 1 can of broth plus two cans of water.

Debbie Gatson - Crockpot red beans are easy and very affordable. It can be a complete meal adding the right amount of sausage. Just cook a pot of cornbread and enjoy!

2 bags red beans
3 cans chicken broth
3 cans water
1/2 cup Badia
1/4 cup garlic
1/4 cup onion powder
1 small onion
1-2 bell peppers or use bag 3 color pepper blend
2 ropes your fav sausage
2 pkg Sazon Goya

Wash 2 bags red beans place in crock pot. Pour in 3 cans of chicken broth and 3 cans water. Add in bag of peppers and dice onion 2 Pkgs of Goya. Cook 2-3 hours. Cut up ropes of sausage and add to pot. Cook 2 more hours. If beans need more fluid add an addtl can of broth and 1 addtl can of water. Cook until soft and fragrant. Enjoy video 8/12/21 & 8/29/21 fb Get Cooking with Debbie G

Pan Fried Crackling Cornbread with Sausage Cabbage

Get Cooking with Debbie G

Crackling hot water Cornbread
1 1/2 cup Corn meal
2 TB soft butter
2 tsp sugar
1 tsp salt
1 tsp baking powder
1 cup hot water
1/2 cup of regular cracklings or chicken cracklings

Cabbage
1 sm cabbage
1/2 purple onion
1 sm cup carrots

Mix all your cornbread ingredients from above and slowly fold in hot water. Start with 1/2 cup and use remainder if needed. Batter should be thick and soft not too runny. I use a bowl with a pouring sprout to mix. Get vegetable grease hot and pour batter like a pancake and brown each side. Place on paper towels when complete.

Cut your small cabbage into small strips. Cut up your 1/2 onion. Put 1 stick butter in a wok and add onions and sausage then add carrots for 5 min then put in cabbage and cook to your liking. Video fb 9/21/21 Get Cooking with Debbie G.

Number of Servings: 4-5

Prep Time: 30

Desserts, Pies, Cakes and Cookies

OVEN TEMPERATURE CHART

Low	250-325F
Moderate	325-375F
Moderate Hot	375-425F
Hot	425-450F
Very Hot	450-475F

TEMPERATURES FOR BAKING FLOUR MIXTURES

FOOD	**Temp.**	**Time**
Butter Cake, loaf	360-400F	40-60 min.
Butter Cake, layer	380-400F	20-40 min.
Cake, fruit	275-325F	3-4 hrs.
Cookies, thin	380-390F	10-12 min.
Cookies, molasses	350-375F	18-20 min.
Cream Puffs	300-350F	45-60 min.
Meringues	250-300F	40-60 min.
Pie Crust	400-500F	20-40 min.

CAKES	**Temp.**	**Time**
Angel	325F	60 min.
Sponge	325F	60 min.
Cup	350F	25 min.
Layer	375F	25-30 min.
Loaf	350F	45-60 min.
Sheet	375F	20-30 min.
Pound	325F	60-90 min.

PIES	**Temp.**	**Time**
Pumpkin	400F	35-45 min.
Two-crust	400F	25-40 min.
Shells	450F	10-12 min.
Meringue	300F	10-15 min.

Blueberry Pancake Bundt

Get Cooking with Debbie G

2 cups fresh blueberries
2 pls Pioneer Pancake mix
2 cups milk
Bakers Joy Nonstick Spray

Preheat oven 350. Spray your Bundt pan. Place 2 cups blueberries at bottom of pan. Mix the two Pkgs of pancake mix with 2 cups milk. Pour mixture over the blueberries. Place in oven snd bake 32 minutes. Remove from oven and drizzle honey and butter over your Pancake Bundt Cake. Great 4 diabetics. Get Cooking with Debbie G.2/21

Quick Brunch Biscuits

Get Cooking with Debbie G

1 can 8 Flaky biscuits
3 TB fresh or frozen blueberries
8 slices of butter
Mini nonstick loaf pan (8)
Nonstick spray

Optional
To make shrimp brunch biscuits substitute shrimp for blueberries. Sauté the shrimp with onions and mushrooms. You can substitute any berry or fruit preserve in middle. Regular fruit would need to be cooked in pan with butter and brown sugar until soft.

Spray your pan with nonstick spray. Divide biscuit in half and press down in pan. Place Tb blue berries with a slice of butter. Place other half of biscuit over and place a slice of butter on top. Do all pans the same or do the shrimp mixture or even a crumble bacon mixture. The brunch biscuits are so good. Bake 10-12 minutes. Look at them after 7 min to make sure they are not cooking too fast. Enjoy Get Cooking with Debbie G 2/11/21.

Cherry Surprise

Get Cooking with Debbie G

3 cups heavy whipping cream
1 pkg cream cheese softened
1 stick melted butter
4-5 TB Sugar
1 can cherry pie filing
1 box small vanilla wafers or graham crackers
1 large gallon bag

Place vanilla cookies in bag and use a metal cup or mallet to beat and crumble them. You can use blender but you usually loose a lot that stick to the blades. Spray small Pyrex dish with no stick spray. Mix graham crumbs, 1/2 cup sugar and butter and press to bottom of dish. keep 1/2 cup to sprinkle on top of dessert later. Pour in 2 cans of cherry pie filling. Make sure cream cheese is softened. Take the 3 cups heavy cream and beat with mixer adding a Tb sugar at a time until soft peaks are formed. Then add the softened cream cheese. Beat together until mixed and it's soft and creamy. Pour mixture over cherry filling and sprinkle graham crackers over top. Refrigerate an hour and enjoy. Get Cooking with Debbie G

Miscellaneous

TEN COMMANDMENTS FOR GOOD LIVING

1. ***SPEAK TO PEOPLE*** - THERE IS NOTHING SO NICE AS A CHEERFUL WORD OF GREETING.

2. ***SMILE AT PEOPLE*** - IT TAKES 72 MUSCLES TO FROWN AND ONLY 14 TO SMILE.

3. ***CALL PEOPLE*** - THE SWEETEST MUSIC TO ANYONE'S EARS IS THE SOUND OF HIS/HER OWN NAME.

4. ***BE FRIENDLY*** AND HELPFUL, IF YOU WOULD HAVE FRIENDS, BE A FRIEND.

5. ***BE CORDIAL*** - SPEAK AND ACT AS IF EVERYTHING YOU DO IS A GENUINE PLEASURE.

6. ***BE GENUINELY*** INTERESTED IN PEOPLE - YOU CAN LIKE ALMOST EVERYBODY IF YOU TRY.

7. ***BE GENEROUS*** WITH PRAISE AND CAUTIOUS WITH CRITICISM.

8. ***BE CONSIDERATE*** WITH THE FEELINGS OF OTHERS. THERE ARE USUALLY THREE SIDES TO A CONTROVERSY; YOURS, THE OTHER PERSON'S AND THE RIGHT SIDE.

9. ***BE ALERT*** TO GIVE SERVICE - WHAT COUNTS MOST IN LIFE IS WHAT WE DO FOR OTHERS.

10. ***ADD TO THIS*** A GOOD SENSE OF HUMOR, A BIG DOSE OF PATIENCE PLUS A DASH OF HUMILITY AND YOU WILL BE REWARDED MANY FOLD.

2 Minute Microwave Omelet

Get Cooking with Debbie G

Breakfast is a very important meal to start your day!! You can't say you don't have enough time for less than 2 minutes of your time. Enjoy your day!

2 eggs
1/8 cup milk
1 TB Badia
Sprinkle of chives
Dash of white pepper
1/2 cup diced cooked chicken breast or bacon
1 TB Pico de Gallo
Butter no stick spray

Spray your small microwave fish with butter pam. Mix all ingredients together place in buttered dish.
Microwave 1.45 min for a soft omelet. More for drier omelet.

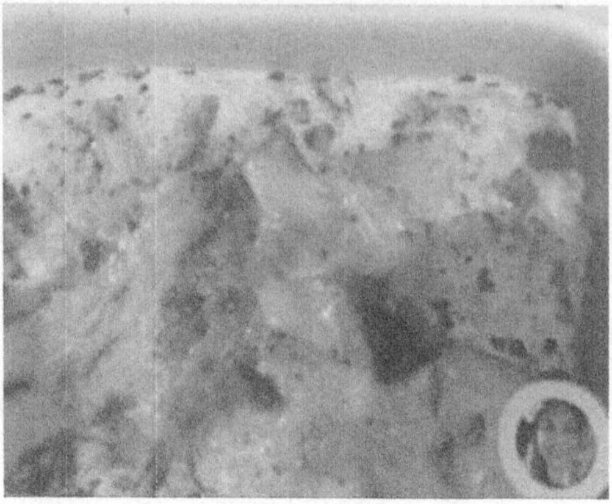

Great Flavor Seasoning for Anything

Get Cooking with Debbie G

1 tsp Smoked Paprika
1 tsp Chili Powder
1/2 tsp garlic powder
1/2 tsp garlic salt with parsley
1/2 tsp onion powder
1/2 tsp Turneric
2Tsp Brown sugar
1 TB Badia Complete Seasoning

Triple ingredients to fill a container for several meals

Mix all your ingredients but tripling saves time.
This recipe has changed over 20 years. It has everything you need for most recipes.

Bacon Sausage Croissant Quiche 12.2k views ★

Get cooking with Debbie G

Easy recipe to make use of old croissants.
12.2 k (thousand)views speaks volumes?

3 Croissants
3 strips bacon
1/2 cup purple onions
1 1/2 cups milk
3 eggs
1 tsp Debbie seasoning or your fav
1 cup sausage
1-2 cups fresh spinach

Fry your bacon until crispy, take out of pan and crumble. Next add purple onions and spinach to the pan and cook until spinach softens. Add bacon and place to the side. Break croissants in pieces. Beat three eggs with 1.5 cups milk and add to croissants. Now add everything together. Spray your pie plate with non stick spray and pour mixture into plate. Make sure you mash the croissants down so all the croissants are covered. Bake at 350 30-35 minutes. Enjoy video 3/15/21 on fb with over 12.2k (thousand) views. Get Cooking with Debbie G

Notes

Notes

Index of Recipes

Order Form

To order additional copies of:

Easy Affordable Cooking 2021

Please contact:

Debbie Gatson
Easy Affordable Cooking 2021 Editor

Get Cooking with Debbie G

ISBN 978-1954262096
9 781954 262096

Made in the USA
Monee, IL
04 November 2026

67374711R00056